I0503494

YOUR INSPIRATIONAL TOOL KIT

How to Move from Being a Dream Chaser to A Dream Catcher
5 powerful tools to help you unlock your inner passion

HARRIETTE GIBBS

Table of Contents

Why did I create the Inspirational Tool Kit?

Well that is easy, we live in a society of so much negativity that it's time for some positivity and inspiration. Don't let the world crush your dreams. This course will guide you through some simple exercises to find your own daily motivation that will help to place you on the path to your own greatness.

I have a couple of quotes that I came up with that inspire me to continue on my path to greatness.

The first quote I like to use is "Change your thoughts, Change your Life-" Harriette Gibbs

My next quote is: "Stop being a Dream Chaser and Become a Dream Catcher-" Harriette Gibbs

Now, let me explain how those quotes have helped me. The first quote truly deals with the mindset. How many times have you attended conferences or read a self- help book that talks about changing your mindset? I'm sure you have heard various leaders say change your mindset a million times.

When you engage in the same behaviors expecting different results that is known as INSANITY. It is time to get in gear and understand that if you want to achieve different results it really begins in the mind. Don't underestimate the Power of the Mind because it is truly a Powerful tool. Think about it, your mindset determines your every move in life good or bad. This is why it is time to put real focus on your mindset because the bottom line is that your mindset will ultimately determine your Great Destiny.

Now, let me explain the importance of the second quote. "Stop being a Dream Chaser and Become a Dream Catcher."

Wow, I love this quote it just resonates with my soul. For so long I have tried so many entrepreneurial opportunities with several multi level marketing companies which finally lead me to creating my own company and capturing my dream. Now, I'm not knocking multi level marketing because this continues to provide me with residual income and one thing that I learned as an entrepreneur is to create MULTIPLE streams of income. However, for me I realized that I had all these wonderful dreams in my mind and I was just sitting on them. In other words I was simply chasing a dream but doing absolutely nothing to capture it. I needed to fix that part of my life it was time to get real and step up to the plate and capture that dream that was birthed inside of me. My vision needed to come to Life!!

Now it's your Turn so let's GET STARTED:

Tool #1 "You Are What You Feed Your Mind"

Write down what you have been feeding your mind good and bad.

1._____

2._____

3._____

4._____

5._____

6._____

7._____

8._____

9._____

10._____

Review your list. What is the main ingredient that you are feeding your mind? Is it good or bad?

If you are feeding your mind good things then congratulations and continue. However, if you are feeding it bad things what are some things you can do today to start changing it? For example, you can begin to do more positive self talk.

Review your list of negative things and begin to change it into a positive affirmation. Let's go.

1._____

2._____

3._____

4._____

5._____

6._____

7._____

8._____

9._____

10._____

Take a minute to reflect on one thing that makes you happy and feel accomplished. What was it and why did it make you feel accomplished or successful?

_____

_____

_____

_____

_____

_____

_____

_____

_____

_____

_____

_____

_____

_____

Think of a time when you wanted to try something brand new but you let fear take over and you didn't pursue it. How did you feel? What was it that made you want to give up? What were the inner voices telling you?

_____

_____

_____

_____

_____

_____

_____

_____

_____

_____

_____

_____

_____

Now it's time for a mind shift. Take the last exercise and turn it around. Think of a time you wanted to try something or pursue a goal and this time FEAR does not win. Write a new scenario of how it would have gone if FEAR weren't a factor. What would you say to those negative inner voices so that you can Push Forward?

_____

_____

_____

_____

_____

_____

_____

_____

_____

_____

_____

_____

_____

Tool #2 Begin to invest in your self-development.

If you are seeking entrepreneurial opportunities or you just want to do some self work to becoming a better you, it's time to set aside some funds to invest in you. Now if you are just starting out that doesn't mean you have to spend an enormous amount of money. Take baby steps and don't get caught up in the social media hype. For instance, on Facebook there may be a ton of people offering coaching services and they may say things like " if you take your business serious you should invest in me." For the new entrepreneur seeing ads like that can be overwhelming and may make you feel that you need to try everybody's program just so you can prove to them and yourself that you are serious. My advice is to choose wisely and know that you simply can't be part of everyone's program. Plus if you did you would be on information overload and talk about frustration, that's exactly what you would be.

I know,I know you have to invest to make money and yes that it is true but you also need

11

to have a roof over your head. You can do things such as create a budget and include a line item for your business or personal development. Look at your budget and determine where you can cut cost and invest more in your business or self development. For instance, can you reduce the number of times you eat out or spend money on entertainment? It's small things that you can do to find the money you need to begin investing in your self-development. Marketing expert, Trevor Otts says, "Invest in yourself at the level in which you expect results." Things that make you go hmmmmm.

Here are a couple of things you can begin investing in and it won't break your bank account:

1. Self-help or Entrepreneurial books
2.   How about this one. Begin to look for FREE webinars or tele- conferences, Yes FREE. There is a wealth of information offered for FREE, all you have to do is look for them. Check out www.callanrush.com,

www.cherylwoodempowers.com,
www.frasernet.com,
www.motivatingthemasses.com,
www.kimflynn.com
www.allysonbyrd.com These websites
offer amazing information and
periodically will share free tele-
conferences or webinars.

3. Check out a local business conference or
   workshop. Here are a couple: Ewomen
   network (www.ewomennetwork.com), or
   Spark and hustle conference
   (www.sparkandhustle.com). Also, check
   out the George Fraser Power networking
   conference.

Think of one thing that you want to improve at
this moment and seek it out. There is a wealth
of information right at your fingertips. When
you can invest in a coach it will make all the
difference in the world. It's all about
profitability and sustainability.

Tool # 3 Know your value

You must realize that you are valuable and bring great value to the table. There is something that is inside of you waiting to be shared with the world and what ever it is know that it has tremendous VALUE. Only you can offer it and no one can duplicate what you bring to the table. So, how do you begin to determine your value? It begins with building your confidence. Stop all of the negative chatter and begin to build yourself up. Realize that you are reaching beyond the stars. Check out your circle of influence known as your friends. Are your friends the ones that encourage your dreams or constantly keep you in that negative place by constantly telling you that your dreams are silly and that you can't do it? Does your circle involve like-minded individuals like you who are striving for greatness and want to make an impact on the world? You have heard the saying "misery loves company," are your friends ones that uplift or love it when you are miserable? Now, this step can be truly tough because it is going to involve a lot of emotion. If you consider someone your friend they have some type of emotional connection to you. So, when you have to evaluate your friendships it may be time to sever some relationships.

Here is your exercise:

Take this time to be quiet and reflect. Go to your favorite room play some soothing music, sit in a comfortable chair, take 10 deep breaths, close your eyes and just reflect for about two or three minutes. Now once you open your eyes begin to write about your friendships and what they mean to you. What do you notice about your friendships? Are you being uplifted or down trodden and be honest with yourself?

_____

_____

_____

_____

_____

_____

_____

_____

_____

15

Now that you have completed this task take a moment because this may have been an emotional time for you. What are you ready to do? Are you ready to disconnect from negative friendships? Do you find yourself always encouraging others and finding that no one is doing that for YOU!! Are you ready to begin transformation?

I am ready to move on from negative friendships because:

_____

_____

_____

_____

_____

_____

_____

_____

_____

_____

Negative Friendships are not meaningful relationships they are toxic and usually only serves the other person. Think about it!! YOU KNOW YOU DESERVE BETTER!!

16

Tool # 4 Get Focused this is your Life and you only get one, so what are you going to do with it?? It is time to do it Big!!

Write down two goals that you want to accomplish this year.

1. _____
   _____
   _____
   _____

2. _____
   _____
   _____
   _____

What will prevent you from accomplishing your goals and why?

_____
_____
_____
_____
_____

Now the real question is will you allow the distractions to deter you from your goals??

Tool # 5 Be Inspired to Move into ACTION!!

Ok, you have identified two goals now let's develop the action steps. What action will you implement to begin to reach your goal?

Goal #1 Action Step:

1._____

_____

_____

_____

_____

_____

_____

Goal #2 Action Step:

1._____

_____

_____

_____

_____

_____

_____

Name two affirmations that you will tell yourself daily to make sure you achieve your goal.

I affirm that_____

_____

_____

_____

_____

_____

I affirm that _____

_____

_____

_____

_____

_____

_____

Create a vision board. A vision board is simply a poster board with your goals and dreams listed on the board or you can cut out pictures and post them to the board. Use magazines to cut out pictures of how you want to design your life. If a vision board seems like too much, consider creating a vision notebook and use post it notes to design your visions. Do what ever is comfortable for you but the bottom line is to write your vision and make it plain. Keep this visual in a place where you can see it often.

Finally, get an accountability partner. An accountability partner will help you stay on task to accomplishing your goal. When you select an accountability partner set a mutual time that you will talk or meet to review your goals.

"How do you catch a Dream? It's simple by moving into intentional Action."- Harriette Gibbs

Suggested Books:
The 10X Rule by Grant Cardone
Profit First by Mike Michalowicz
The Jet Set Girl's Guide to Building a Million Dollar Online Empire by Cheryl Broussard

Take this page and design your life!!

This is how I want my life:_____

_____

_____

_____

_____

_____

_____

_____

_____

_____

_____

_____

_____

_____

_____

_____

_____

_____

_____

_____

_____

_____

Now that you have designed your life close your eyes and reflect on the life you designed. Just imagine actually living it. How does it feel? Where are you living? What does your circle of friends look like now? Think about it!! If you can write it out and imagine it YOU CAN LIVE IT. It's up to you in how you will move toward it.   SO Let's Get it.

The Best Gift you can give yourself is an Amazing Life!

BONUS

As you continue on your journey think about ways you can generate income with your business ideas.

For instance think about your idea for a business.

What is the idea_____

What are some of the products you can create? For example, write a book, create a cd, create a workbook etc.

1._____

_____

2._____

_____

What are some of the services that you can offer? For example, tele-seminars, webinars, live workshops, e-course etc.

1. _____

2. _____

3. _____

Look at the list you have created and begin to think of the one product you can create before the end of the year.

Be creative and go for it!! Make this your year to break out of the FEAR mode. I recently saw a quote that read, "F-E-A-R has two meanings, Forget Everything And Run or Face Everything And Rise the choice is yours."- ANON

So, what choice will you make? Remember it's time to become a *"Dream Catcher."* I hope the tools were helpful and that you will implement them. You are worth it and you need to share your wonderful dreams with the world someone out there needs you!!!!

Do the work so that you can live the life that many people only dream of!!!

Remember BE INSPIRED!

Here's to your Success!!

25

www.ingramcontent.com/pod-product-compliance
Lightning Source LLC
Chambersburg PA
CBHW080631180526

45168CB00007B/3124